8 Easy Steps to Sell Your Own HDB Flat

8 Easy Steps to Sell Your Own HDB Flat

Beginners Guide to Sell Like a Pro

Shahlan S Shahlan

PARTRIDGE

A Penguin Random House Company

Library of Congress Control Number: 2014949046
ISBN: Hardcover   978-1-4828-2688-3
               Softcover   978-1-4828-2687-6
               eBook   978-1-4828-2689-0

To order additional copies of this book, contact
Toll Free 800 101 2657 (Singapore)
Toll Free 1 800 81 7340 (Malaysia)
orders.singapore@partridgepublishing.com

www.partridgepublishing.com/singapore

Preface

I thank Allah daily for making this book possible. Writing a book has always been a goal for me for the past many years since I became self-employed, and I believe for most of us.

It was not until I attend "The Publish A Book & Grow Rich Bootcamp" in 2013 by Gerry Robert that really got me to sit down and started writing this book.

A few weeks later in April 2013, nearly 80% of this book is written.

However, the Singapore authorities then has just started to introduce one of the many cooling measures to discourage speculative activity.

There were also a growing number of real estate agents who have started to experience lower activity and lesser income. I decided not to publish this book then because my intention might be interpreted wrongly.

Looking back, it is a wise decision as there are many important fundamental changes since then in relation to the topic of this book. Looking forward, there will still be more changes but most of the contents will still be relevant in many more years to come.

Foreword

Selling your HDB flat is one of the major decisions you'll make in your lifetime. For some people, it causes stress and discomfort to themselves and their family members.

The good news is that YES, you can sell it yourself. It is not a requirement by HDB to engage a real estate consultant. In fact, about 1% of sales transaction is done without an agent.

This guidebook is written for people just like you – the DIY seller.

This book may also be useful for new real estate agents or even experienced agents who is not familiar in HDB transactions.

If you are engaging the services of a qualified real estate agent who can provide value to you, please ask your agent to BUY this book for you.

To make this guide book simple and easy to understand, I will only touch on selling the house in a straight forward case.

The whole process of looking for a buyer till the HDB completion date (also known as the 2nd apt) in which you will have to move out of the house is around 3-6 mths, depending on the time you have a willing buyer agreeing to your price.

Therefore, you shall plan the timing and have some flexibility in it.

Even though this book is titled "8 Easy Steps to Sell Your HDB Flat", I have divided the book into 12 chapters.

However, there is only 8 main steps to sell your flat:-

1. Checking your Eligibility & Financial Calculation
2. Marketing Your Flat
3. Answering Enquiries
4. Dressed Up Your Flat
5. Show Time
6. Negotiation & Closing
7. Paperwork & Submission
8. HDB Appointments

I hope you find the information useful and the examples and tips entertaining and can provide value to you.

Happy Reading!
Happy Selling!

By
S Shahlan
Real Estate Salesperson

CHAPTER 1

WHY? – the objective

Now that you are thimking of selling your flat, you need to ask yourself a question before you proceed.

WHY am I selling my flat? What is my **OBJECTIVE?**

There are few possible reasons:-

Unlock the POSITIVE EQUITY (cash or profits) in your flat

Using the cash proceeds to start a business

Using the profits to buy an overseas property

Investments in other asset classes e.g unit trusts, forex

Investments in other real estate classes e.g industrial, commercial

Moving to a preferred location (e.g near workplace, choice of schools, parent's home)

Buying a bigger flat to accommodate additional family members/ grown up children

Buying a smaller flat because the children have moved out

Buying another flat to reduce the loan

Paying in full for the next house

Upgrading to a private property

Staying with children

Migrating

And many others…..

I suggest **you write these reasons at this box**

MY OBJECTIVE IN SELLING MY FLAT

There is a reason why I want you to write it down, which I will tell you later.

CHAPTER 2

PRICE – How much to sell?

The million dollar question?

You heard your neighbour sold their flat for $500,000 and you probably want $20K or $50K more to have that bragging rights.

Price your unit too high and you would have many calls without any viewing.

You may also have many people coming to view your flat but without any offer. Your flat will be like a museum.

Your high price will also help your competitors house to be sold first.

Price too low and you will regret forever.

Before you decide on an appropriate selling price, you can check from these few sources to determine your selling price:-

1. HDB Resale Flat Prices

http://services2.hdb.gov.sg/webapp/BB33RTIS/BB33PReslTrans. jsp

or Google 'HDB resale past transaction'.

This shows you the recent transacted prices of HDB flats, up to the past 12 months.

How to?

a. **FLAT TYPE, select the type of your flat e.g 5 room**

b. **HDB TOWN, select your town.**

c. **Skip to RESALE REGISTRATION DATE, select the past 3 month e.g May 2014 to July 2014.**

d. **CLICK 'I Accept".**

The data generated will give you an indication the price of the flats already sold in your estate for the past few months.

You could probably see the difference between the highest and the lowest transacted prices is about $20,000 to $50,000. This is probably due to the different types of model available in your town. The other difference could also be the level or floors, the floor area or sqm2, and the age of the block. This data could be seen clearly.

All things being equal, sometimes the difference could also be much because the flat that fetches the higher price could probably have a good orientation, a very good view or a 'designer decor' interior.

2.   Centralised Map Services

On the same main page, click on <u>HDB Centralised Map Services</u>.

<u>http://services2.hdb.gov.sg/web/fi10/emap.html#</u>

Alternatively, you can check past transactions of HDB flats within 500 metres of your flat. However, this data shows all the different types of flats prices.

3. Property portals available on the internet.

You can do a search and look at the selling price posted on the web.

4. Newspaper advertisement.

Buy the Straits Times on a Saturday.

For (3) and (4) call up everyone selling the same type of flat in your area. Make enquires as though you are looking and buying a flat. Get the following details:-

Selling price, area in sqm, which level, corner/corridor, orientation, last offer (if any)

Now that you know the recent transacted price and the price current sellers are asking, you would probably have decided on a selling price.

WRITE IT DOWN HERE

$_____ (as this is for calculation purpose, decide on a realistic and conservative figure)

The price depends on the market.

In a **buyer's market** where there are more sellers than buyers, a well renovated high floor flat opposite the MRT could probably be sold at the valuation price or even below it.

Sellers would sometimes get frustrated because there would be no offers even if they have lowered their asking price.

In a **seller's market** where there are many buyers than sellers, an original condition low floor unit could sometimes be sold at a price higher than the valuation price.

Which market are you in now?

Chapter 3

Financial Calculation

Now this is one of the most important part because the amount of cash proceeds or profits (if any) will influence your decision if you were to proceed with your plan.

To calculate and see if there is any cash from this sales, you need:-

A – Selling Price

B – Outstanding Loan (HDB, bank, or no loan)

C – (Seller 1) CPF amount to be Refunded

D – (Seller 2) CPF amount to be Refunded

How to get these info/data?

A

This is the selling price that we have discussed in the previous chapter. As this is for calculation purpose, use a conservative figure.

B

If you don't have any loan, please enter $0 at B. If you have a loan, please check the outstanding amount from the **bank or HDB**.

1. HDB Loan

Go to http://www.hdb.gov.sg/

Or Google "outstanding HDB loan"'

Go to Living in HDB flats

Go to Mortgage Loan

Click on View More ......

Click on Mortgage Loan Statement

Go to Retrieve your Mortgage Loan Statement via Online e-Service

Click on "Statement of Account for Mortgage Loan."

Log in via your SingPass.

Click on My Flat.

At the right side, you will see Purchased Flats.

Below it, click on Financial Information.

You can now see your Outstanding Balance. This is the figure you need for B.

Bank Loan

Get this info from your bank. Call and ask them to send over the statement.

C

D

(the figures for the above C and D is for 2 owners of the same flat. If the flat has 1 owner, then you'll use C only)

Go to CPF website http://mycpf.cpf.gov.sg/Members/home.htm

Or google "CPF Board"

Log in with your ID and SingPass

On your left side, at My CPF Online Services, click at My Statement

Go to Section C (Net Amount Used & Amount Available)

Click on Property

Click on My Public Housing Withdrawal Details

Look at the figure (Total principal amount withdrawn and accrued interest)

This is the figure you need for C and D.

If there are more than 2 people who contribute in paying for your flat using their CPF, please repeat the above steps to check on the figures for the extra paying individuals.

Now that you have these 4 figures, do this simple calculation (subtract them) :-

A (Selling Price) -B (Outstanding Loan) - C (Seller 1 CPF amount to be refunded) - D (Seller 2 CPF amount to be refunded)

e.g

A $500,000

B $80,000

C $120,000

D $100,000

Therefore the cash proceeds is $200,000.

Chapter 4

Eligibility to Sell ?

Minimum Occupation Period (MOP)

After you've done your financial calculation and now that you are excited about selling your place for a good profit, you have to check with the HDB if you are eligible to sell your flat.

You must have physically occupied your flat for a period of time before you are eligible to sell it in the open market. This period is known as the Minimum Occupation Period (MOP).

This period will depend on the flat type, when you bought the flat and the purchase mode (loan or no loan).

Generally, you have to physically occupied your flat for 5 years.

How to check your MOP?

Google "HDB certificate of eligibility to sell"

1. Click on HDB InfoWEB e-Service : Computation of Occupation Period ...

https://services2.hdb.gov.sg/webapp/BP21NonPortalWeb/jsp/non-portal/BP21PEligibilitytoSell.jsp

2. Fill up the required information. HDB will send you a letter within 2 weeks.

3. Do keep this letter.

4. However, do take note that even if the letter states that you are eligible to sell your flat, it doesn't means that your resale application (if you do have a buyer) is approved because that is subject to the resale policy prevailing at the point of application.

Race Quota (Ethnic Integration Policy)
and Permanent Resident quota

This is an important step before you market your flat. You have to check if any race of buyers or permanent residents (SPR) cannot buy your flat. This becomes an issue in certain areas where there is a larger concentration of a particular race.

How to check?

Google "HDB race quota" and click on

Ethnic Integration Policy and SPR Quota – HDB

http://services2.hdb.gov.sg/webapp/BB29ETHN/BB29STREET

1. Fill up your particulars. And click on "I Accept". Results will be immediate.

If you can sell your flat to all race and all SPRs, congratulations. This means you have a wider market of potential buyers to sell to.

If you can't sell to any particular race, do let the potential buyers and agents know before they turn up to view your flat.

The SPR quota and ethnic proportions are updated on the 1st of every month. So please do keep yourself updated.

If you belong to a minority race e.g Malay, Indian or Others (e.g Eurasian, Filipinos, etc), and you can only sell to your own race, you would probably take a longer time to sell especially in areas where not much of your own community wanted to buy and reside there.

I recall a listing I had many years ago in Bishan where only Malay buyers can buy the flat. The listing expired in 3 months with 1 good offer that the owner didn't accept. It was then marketed by another 2 agents before it came back to me 6 months later. By the time it was sold, it took a year from the time I first met the owner and discuss about selling his flat.

Currently at the time of writing, I am selling a flat near Holland Village where the valuation of the 5 room flat is $785K. The only eligible buyers are non-Chinese.

Once a Chinese couldn't buy your flat, more than 80% of potential buyers couldn't buy your flat. This also means that when a genuine offer is made, you should seriously consider taking the offer (as long as the price is reasonable). Don't expect the buyer to pay a high premium as the buyer themselves will probably face the same situation when he wants to sell his flat in the future.

CHAPTER 5

Resale Checklist

The Resale Checklist provides a list of HDB's policies and procedures that you should be aware of before you sell your flat.

You have to go through the Resale Checklist before you start to market your flat for sale. Only one of the sellers will need to submit the checklist by logging in with his/ her NRIC number and SingPass.

How to?

Google " resale checklist for seller"

http://services2.hdb.gov.sg/webapp/BB24ResaleChecklistBS/BB24SHome

Near the bottom of the page

Click on Submit New Checklist

Please follow the instructions stated at the HDB website.

Using your SingPass, you will be required to fill up the standard personal particulars e/g. name, IC, email, contact number.

You will also be required to read the list and acknowledged it by ticking the required boxes.

You have to state your next housing option e.g if you buying another flat, or staying with a relative, etc.

You may be required to indicate the address of the place you are going to stay. If you buying another resale flat, you have to submit a financial plan.

Upon completion of the Seller Resale Checklist, you must observe the 7 day cooling-off period before you grant the OTP.

It means you may sell your flat **7 days later.** The resale checklist is valid for 6 months.

After the resale checklist expire, you have to re-do another checklist again.

CHAPTER 6

Marketing Your Flat

Determine a good time to list your home. Slow months are from December to February. It is quite common for Singaporeans to travel at the end of the year around the December school holidays. And around February, there is the Chinese New Year. However, this does not means that there is no activity.

The month of July can also be slow because of the Hungry Ghost month.

You will have to come up with a marketing plan. Different forms of marketing have different costs, effectiveness and objectives.

I suggest you do most or all of these things:-

1. advertise in the local **newspaper.**

2. advertise in the local internet property portals.

3. print and distribute **flyers.**

4. sms to other property agents.

What is the information prospective buyer wants to know?

1. Block number

2. estate/town.

3. Flat type or model e.g 5A, 3NG

4. floor level e.g low, mid, high or ground

5. orientation (facing east or north, etc)

6. state of the house (move-in condition, original, well-renovated)

You may not want to reveal everything in your chosen marketing medium as you may want interested parties to call you to ask about these details, so you can gauge the level of interest in your flat. At this stage, I would like to remind you that your flat unit number is confidential.

Please do not state a feature that your flat does not have. This is misrepresentation and may cause legal complications later on.

Photos

You may want to include photos. Please do take as many photos as you can from many angles and choose around 3 that looks really good only to be included in the advertisement. The reason you shouldn't be putting too many photos is because you don't want to show everything that there is no need for buyers to come and view.

You should include photos in the online advertisement and flyers. If your house is simply renovated or in original condition, do not put any photos of the interior of your flat. You may want to show photos of the surrounding amneties e.g shops, malls, MRT, playground, parks, etc.

However, putting photos of your flat interior in the newspaper advertisement is very costly. As such, not many sellers and agents do this. However, I'm not stopping you to do this.

How to advertise?

1) Newspaper - Cats

Call 1800 2899988 Mon-Fri from 8.30am to 6.30pm for assistance or go to http://www.cats.com.sg/default/bookyourads

It cost around $11 per line for RUN-ON ads. (RUN-ON ads is the 3 or 4 line ads that you usually see in the papers). You have to use 3 lines minimum. So the average cost is $35.31 including GST. If you advertise 3 times weekly, that would work out to $1,377.09 for the next 3 months.

To be more effective, I suggest you use a 4 liner. However, the costs will be $1,836.12 if you advertise 3 times a week for the next 3 months.

Use the following words in your ad if your flat has such features:-

Unblock, sea view, city view, nice view, 120 sqm (the floor area), breezy, bright, corner unit, well- renovated, designer deco, modern deco, move-in, near MRT, schools, shops, food courts, amneties, all races (eligibility of races).

2) Internet

As around 72% of Singaporeans uses the internet, this medium have a better chance of reaching more people.

These are few examples of the internet portals where you can advertise and market your flat.

a) ST Property

http://www.stproperty.sg/user/userad/createad

b) Nation Property

http://www.nationproperty.sg/

3) Flyers

If you print flyers, you can use the services of the flyer printers to distribute them. There are a few modes of distribution.

1. HDB Door to Door Distribution

2. Walkway Handouts

3. Letterbox Distribution.

Do call the flyer distributors for the rates.

Alternatively, you can distribute these flyers yourselves. You could put the flyers at the door or gate on each flat in your block and the surrounding neighbourhood.

These owners could probably know someone who is looking to buy a flat in your block because their parents or their children wants to buy a flat in your area. You could also distribute them at the nearest market or at the MRT station in your estate. Please check if you need the necessary approval from the relevant authorities before you proceed to distribute at the premises that I've mentioned.

However, distributing flyers yourself is not time-effective unless you are unemployed or a full time house-husband or housewife. Therefore, I suggest you use the services of the flyer distributions.

4) SMS to property agents

Do this on Saturday morning.

You will notice that there are many agents advertising their flat for sale in your estate. List down their names and contact numbers. Sms them your flat details.

E.g

Hi, I am selling my own flat. Details:-

Blk 999 Holland Village 5I High floor corner. Renovated, move-in condition. Unblock city view. Bright and breezy. North South facing. Near MRT and amneties. $500,000 nego.

If you have any buyer, please bring them over.

5) Others

There are many other ways of marketing. This could be promoting your flat on social media e.g FaceBook. You could also tell your friends about your flat. Some malls have a advertisement board where you can put an ad for free.

Selling a home is about exposure, so anything that will expose your flat to more people is beneficial.

CHAPTER 7

Answering Those Calls

This is the most crucial apart. Whether you are an employee or self employed, you have to be in a position that you can **pick up and answer** all those enquires that will be coming in. You can't be working in a location where there is no mobile network, or you can't answer calls whilst working.

90% of these calls will be from property agents. Their questions will be direct and brief and it is easier to talk to them. They are busy people. They know what they want. It will be around 1-2 minutes only.

Q: " Hi Mr……. good morning, may I co-broke your 5 room Blk 111? May I know what is the asking price? Is the price nego (negotiable?) What floor is this? Open to all races? When can view?

A: Hi, we are asking for $540K only. This is on the mid floor. Yes, its open to all races. Viewing can be arranged most of the time, mostly on weekends and weekday nights. There is viewing today."

For direct buyers who is experienced, they may know what to ask. But an inexperienced buyer take a longer time to entertain. They will sometimes loss their thoughts and words.

They will still ask the same type of questions but in a different manner. You have to be patient with them.

Q: Hi, you're selling Blk 111?

A: Yes.

Q: So how much are you selling?

A: $540K.

Q: How much is the last transaction?

A: $500K.

Q: So, you're selling above the market price? Why so expensive?

A: ....

Most of the times, the call will lasts longer than usual.

Your Objective Have to Be Clear

NEVER negotiate price over the phone, regardless if it's a direct buyer or an agent. If you are marketing your flat at a realistic price, at the market price or just slightly above the market price, the price shouldn't be an issue at this stage.

Your main objective of entertaining these enquires is to feed them with some information that will get them excited wanting to **come and view your flat**. Then only you have a chance of a buyer to like your house and want to buy it.

Answer these calls with a smile. You are now a salesperson – selling your own flat. Your voice is the first impression of your flat.

Practise answering these enquires with your family members before the very first call. Answer those calls in front of a mirror. Remember to smile. A person who smiles whilst answering calls sounds genuine and friendly. Salespeople and tele- marketeers do this!

Very Important Note: Never give your unit number or even the level of your flat. Without making any appointment, they might loiter around your flat trying to take a peek into your unit.

Viewing Time?

Most prospective buyers will want to view on weekends and weekday nights. Occassionally, you will have request for viewing on a weekday during office hours. The usual timing is 7-9.30 pm on weekdays and 1-6pm on Saturday and Sunday. However, the timing will be determined by you.

How to arrange the viewing?

Lets say your flat is in a popular area and you are selling in a "seller's market", there will be many people wanting to view your flat. And you have decided that the viewing time is between 2-4pm. Try to space the time between those buyers at 20 minutes interval e.g 2.40pm, 3pm, 3.20 pm, 3.40pm.

Most people will view your flat between 4-10 minutes. Unless they are very interested, they will usually leave within 5 minutes.

(if it is a jumbo flat or maisonette, some may takes about 15-20 minutes.)

The 20 minutes difference between each viewing is to have some buffer or allowance. Because quite often, there are buyers who will be late because they could possibly be held up in another viewing, or the agent's buyer got caught in the traffic jam, and so on.

Some buyers would call a few days earlier to arrange a viewing. There could also be cancellations for some of these viewings.

Some will give a 1 hour notice. You decide if you want to grant the last minute request.

From experience, the best is 1 day before, or the morning on the same day before the afternoon viewing.

Call by property agents

You could also be "harassed" by property agents wanting to sell your property. A few days after you start to market your own flat, your listing will ends up in a database meant for real estate agents. Your flat will be classified as FSBO (for sale by owners). There are many new agents and some experienced property agents without a house to sell, and they will call you to offer their services.

Some other Enquires

At times, you may have some enquires. Some buyers would like to know the facing of the door.

Indian buyers would like to know the total of the numbers of your unit number. Suppose your unit number is #03-346. You have to add the numbers 0+3+3+4+6. The total is 16. So you let the interested buyer or the agent knows the total number. You don't have to let them know your unit number.

CHAPTER 8

Dressed For Success

Although I have placed this chapter late into the book, you should consider doing some of these things earlier. As cleaning up your place can be done in stages, you should do this once you've decided to sell your flat.

1. Spend a little bit of money to do up your place. Some sellers think that minor repairs are not necessary. Minor repairs and minimal spending can make a lot of difference.

2. An example is to give your house a fresh coat of paint. If you last paint your house a few years back or you have children scribbling on your walls, do this. A new coat of paint and the smell will give the buyers a feeling of buying something new. Buyers like the 'new' factor although they may re-paint it to their choice of colours after they purchase your flat.

However, do avoid painting the front door and the gate. This will make your buyer suspicious of loan-shark activities.

3. Clean your house throughout, from top to bottom. And especially the areas where there is heavy usage e.g the kitchen, wash areas and the toilets.

4. Clear up clutter while you clean. Buyers want to feel like they are buying sufficient space. So clear all the unnecessary junks so as to make your house look spacious. If you have a furniture that you can do without now and are not bringing to your new place or your temporary accommodation, sell or give it to someone.

    Or call your HDB town council to arrange for a free disposal.

5. Put away your least-used items such as toys, gym equipments, blenders, etc.

6. If your lights is a bit dim, change them. A bright light will make the flat looks spacious and enhance details in your flat.

7. You may also consider taking family photos down. The less personal your home is, the easier it is for the buyers to

visualize themselves living in it. You should seriously consider to remove religious items.

8. If your house do not have an air con system or a water heater or anything that is very costly, do not buy these items even though they will enhance the appeal of the flat. There are some buyers who might want to tear up your place and replace everything if they buy over your place.

9. Whatever you do, your objective here is to make the house as pleasing to the buyer's eyes and liveable as possible with minimum spending.

CHAPTER 9

Showtime

So a few prospective buyers are coming to view your flat today. Are you ready for the show?

1. On the day of viewing, roll down the blinds and draw out the curtains to make your house looks bright. This is especially important if your house have an excellent view, maybe of greenery or the city skyline.

2. If you do have a dark spot in your house, do switch on the lights in that part of the house.

3. Open the windows if there is breeze. If it is a hot day, switch on the air con about 30 minutes before the first person comes. These buyers may be in between viewings of other units and

they are probably tired and thirsty. They may even stay a bit longer as a cold room will bring relief to them.

4. If you have pets, removed them from the house or put them in their cages. Not all buyers are pet lovers, and the mere glimpse of your beloved pets can make them not wanting to step into the house.

5. If possible, do not have other family members in the house, especially noisy children. The lesser people in the house, the better it is.

6. Put all your personal valuables locked in a safe place.

7. When these buyers or agents reaches your block, they would normally call you. Since you will be waiting in your flat, give them your unit number.

   (Property agents would usually wait for their co-broke agents or buyers at the void deck. On the way to your flat, they would engage in small banter, and usually took the opportunity to explain the amneties around the area.)

8. Welcome them graciously.

9. Show them around the flat. You have to lead them. If your flat is a big flat (e.g jumbo or maisonette) and it's a party of four and above, sometimes they like to wander off in different directions. Take charge.

10. In that split second, you have to be able to sense which part of the house they would like to see first. Most women would like to see the kitchen first, so lead them there.

11. Do not mention "this is the kitchen, this is the bedroom" and so on. It's very obvious. Even a 5 year old kid can do that.

12. Bring out the selling points in your house e.g " this kitchen cabinet is 8 years old, but as you can see its look as new as we clean it every day." "We service the air con every 3 months", and so on. I've seen some really good agents that they can explain things that you can't see.

13. Be enthuastic and helpful. You have to pass on your positive energy. The stage now belongs to you.

14. Identify the parts of the house which the buyer likes most. They tend to stay there longer. These are known as Sweet Spots. Let them absorb the atmosphere.

15. Sometimes, they are standing a few metres away and staring at a certain spot. These buyers have some plans for their interior decoration and are now thinking if buying this flat would fit in with their plans. Speak to them as though as they are now owning this property.

16. If they are discussing among the family members or with their agents, back off to give them some privacy. They may have some issues and may not want to offend you in case you hear. However, in this case, you don't have a chance to answer this objections should they not bring this up later. After allowing them some private time, approach them and ask if they have any concerns.

17. Observe buying signals. If they ask many questions, it is an indication that they are interested. They may ask about the surrounding schools, public transport services, food centres. This is one of the many buying signals.

Above all, be enthuastic and helpful. You have to pass on your positive energy. You should rehearse showing your flat many times before the first viewing. Have you ever been to a 1 hour play? These actors spent probably more than 20 hours rehearsing for that 1 hour show. Your flat is now your stage.

<u>Security Issues You Should Take Note</u>

If a direct buyer calls to view, you have to qualify the buyer during the phone call. There could be some criminals taking advantage of showhouses by direct owners just like you.

Have more than 1 man in the house, if possible. Inform your neighbours that you have buyers coming over and to keep an open eye and ear for your place.

Don't close the main gate and door, in case you need a quick escape. Have the telephone numbers of these direct buyers in a file.

Whereas possible, have their car description or licence plate jot down.

Follow Up

After the viewing for the day is over, try to remember the faces to the names of the people that have come. The next day, contact these prospective buyers and ask them what they thought of your flat. Some will mention that they are thinking, deciding, or have arranged to view some other flats before making a decision.

You could possibly have a very keen party that is interested to buy your flat. But because of your follow-up call, that buyer becomes more interested. Some buyers simply needs to be pushed and nudged a little bit.

I don't understand that there are quite a number of real estate agents who don't practice these.

CHAPTER **10**

Negotiation and Some Closing Techniques

You can allow the deal to close by itself or you can play a part in being pro- active and influence a buyer to buy your flat. Encourage your buyer to make an offer.

This is where your negotiation skills come in handy.

Hundreds of books have been written on this topic alone. I cannot summarize everything that I learnt from the past many years that is involved in this dynamic, often-complex strategy in one single chapter.

Negotiation is when you try to Compete and Co-operate at the same time. It also involves trying to influence an outcome.

In today's litigious society, we often see people enter into negotiations with the belief that it has to be a negative, confrontational experience. The other party does not have to be your enemy. The objective here is to be a "win-win" situation for all parties involved.

Generally, humans are kind, helpful and reasonable. However when it comes to negotiation, everyone wants to be the winner.

Show the buyer you are reasonable, and the chances are very good that he will show you the same.

There Have to be some Friction!

However, it doesn't mean that when the buyer offers you your asking price, you accept it immediately. On the surface, a negotiation that starts smoothly and ends quickly without too much hassle appears to be a good one. But it isn't necessarily true.

Do you remember the time when you negotiate and the other party quickly accept your asking price immediately, you feel that you didn't get as good a deal as you could have. The other party didn't put up too much resistance. They were happy to accept your offer, and you feel you got the worse end.

The truth is, the other party probably feels the same way. The deal looks too easy. And you often find in these type of negotiations that go quickly and smoothly is that one or both parties wants to back out of the deal.

Remember, in any successful negotiation, both parties will have to come out of it the victorious. It is also about ego and pride.

Information is Power!

When a buyer comes to view, it is important to get as much information about them as possible.

That buyer may be looking for a flat in your block, or in the neighbourhood only. The schools their children attended to is just around the corner, or their parents looking after their children is staying there.

These are what we called 'genuine buyers' and they are willing to pay your price. They don't have much choice. They have waited for a few months or probably a year for a seller in your area.

Or another buyer could have just sold his flat and have to buy another flat within 2 weeks. Another buyer is getting married and has to buy a flat soon.

This information will let you access their sincerity of buying a flat.

Remember to write all these information because you would probably have many potential buyers coming and couldn't remember these facts.

Get your buyer to commit the price first.

Buyer: What's your best offer?

You: Do you like my flat?

Buyer: Sort of....... But what's your best price?

You: If you like the house and really wants to buy it, we can always discuss about the price. Do you like this flat?

Buyer: Yes. But what's the best price?

You: If you like my place, what's the best you can offer?

Buyer: (paused and discuss with spouse) Our best price is $490,000.

You: Is that the best you can offer?

Buyer: Yes

You: So if I'm offering you $491,000, you won't buy it.

(wait for respond- they could probably come up with a higher figure)

Buyers or with their agents do employ many kinds of strategies when it comes to negotiating. These are the few of them:-

1. "lowball offer"

Don't take this personally. Sometimes, buyers have to prove to themselves and to get the exclusive bragging rights that they have the best deal ever. We all have friends like this. If the buyer could see that you are not going to let them "steal" your flat, they would accept the reality and increase their offer to something realistic.

(Some buyers and their agents know you that you don't have to pay any comission and will offer you a price that has been reduced by the commission it would have cost to use an agent - effectively eliminating any cost savings.)

2.   Traditional method

Suppose buyer is willing to pay a maximum of $500,000 for your asking price of $530,000, they will start first by offering $470,000. This method is the most common use, and probably the only one used by inexperienced negotiators. The buyer hoped that you will come down and meet them "half-way".

This method would probably work when your asking price is realistic and you would be willing to lower your price. Both sides would appear as "winners".

The disadvantages is that if both parties don't move at the same "pace". Suppose one party moves by $5,000, and the other party moves by $1,000 only. Or one party responds in 1 hour and the other party responds the next day, it can create "ill-feelings". Negotiations can break down.

CLOSING

Now that the buyer have offer you the PRICE that you want, how do you respond? As I mention earlier, do not accept it immediately.

Good guy- The other Guy technique

You use this conversation when they offer the PRICE that you want or when it's just slightly below your PRICE. Depending on the time that you want to respond to them, it is important that your spouse is not there beside you.

"Mr Buyer, I am happy that you like my flat and I would like you to own my flat. However, I will inform my spouse and let her/him know about your offer.

He/She is also a decision maker.

I will let her know that a nice family really wants to buy our flat. Could you give us some time?"

If you want to accept the offer in 5-10 minutes, move away from the buyer and call your spouse immediately, or go to your master bedroom if your partner is there. Stay there for the next 5-10 minutes and comes out to congratulate the buyer.

If you want to accept the offer in 1 hour or the next day, tell them that once your partner returns, you will discuss and let them know.

The advantage of this is that some buyers will be getting anxious and may even increase their offer.

Even if this doesn't happen, and since you have gotten the price that you wanted, call them to come down and close the deal.

(Note: Second hand car dealers loves to use this technique. You have offered their asking price. They will say that they have to call their boss, and they go inside their air-con cubicle 'calling' their boss. A few minutes later, they re-appear and congratulates you.)

So what do you say when you want to close the deal? Have nice things to say about them. You may use this "**Only For You**" conversation:-

"Mr Buyer, since we wanted a higher price, we declined your offer at first. But since we like you and your nice family to owns our nice home, therefore, we have decided to accept your offer. However, this price is for you only".

The 2nd viewing technique.

If a buyer offers you a price that is close to what you want, and you can feel that they can actually offers you your asking PRICE, you can mention that an interested party has offered you your asking price and they are coming later for a 2nd viewing. The buyers will feel the heat from the competition. Naturally, people wants to win. By this time, they are already emotionally attached to your flat and would probably not willing to take the risk of your flat being bought by someone else.

Closing on the very 1st Offer

Don't be afraid to take the first offer. Many times, the first offer is the highest offer.

And quite often, sellers rejected the first offer even though it is good. Sellers thought that the next offer will be higher, and higher. It doesn't work that way!

Do not have Sellers regret!

After your deal is done, you will probably still have calls for your unit. Some may ask you about the selling price. You do not have to reveal it to them. If you did reveal to these buyers, the conversation could go on like these:-

Buyer: Hi, is your flat still available?

You: Sorry it's sold.

Buyer: May I know how much did you sell for?

You: $500,000

Buyer: $500,000 only? I would buy for $530,000!

If a buyer is not eligible to buy your flat, he could also offer a million dollars. This could happen to any sellers or even buyers.

Note : Once, I was selling a Malay house in Queenstown. As the Chinese ratio is filled, the sellers could only sell to a Malay, Indian and Others. There is a Chinese neighbour who happens to know that my seller was selling their flat. He came to knock on the door and offered nearly a million dollar for a flat which is valued at $750,000 only! Do you believe he will really buy at that price if he's qualified to buy the flat?

CONCLUSION

I cannot guarantee you which type of strategies you use will work or fail. Most of the times, you will have to go with the "feel" of the situation.

Do remember that you, as sellers set the price, but it is the buyers that sets the value.

Extra Note:

Sellers of HDB flats (from 22 July 2014) will be able to request from their buyers for a temporary extension of stay in their HDB flats, by up to three months. Sellers who wish to extend their stay must have committed to buy another flat at the time of the resale application, i.e. they must have exercised an Option to Purchase. The request for the extension of stay is to be submitted to HDB at the time of the selling resale application.

It is not the right of sellers to demand this extension. Any such arrangements are subject to the agreement of buyers. This request have to be communicated when you are marketing your flat, as this may affect your selling price. The duration and monetary compensation, if any, must be agreed to by both buyers and sellers.

Important Note to Buyer: Buyers should take note that your Minimum Occupation Period will be affected when you agree to let the seller this temporary extension of stay. Minimum Occupation Period will commences only on the day when you take over the flat. The extension of stay will automatically cease at the end of three months. Any earlier termination must also be communicated to HDB, as this will impact flat buyers' Minimum Occupation Period.

CHAPTER 11

Signing the Option to Purchase

Once both sellers and buyers have agreed on a price, it is time to seal the agreement in writing.

However, there is one more thing that you need to know, even before you start to negotiate the price.

Option and Exercise Fee

As in any real estate transaction, a buyer have to pay you

1. Option fee ($1 to $1,000)
2. Exercise fee

In a HDB Option to Purchase contract, the total of option and exercise fees combined cannot be more than $5,000.

The Option Fee could be a sum between $1 to a maximum of $1,000, to be negotiated between you and the buyer.

Once the Option have been granted, you as the seller cannot give another Option to another buyer until the Option granted expires.

The Option period is 21 calendar days (including Saturday, Sunday and public holidays) from the date of granting the OTP. It expires at 4pm on the 21st calendar day.

The maximum option fee you may collect is $1,000. That means if you have collected $1,000, the maximum exercise fee you collect later is $4,000.

Both of you, the seller and buyer, have to agree to both of the option and exercise fee amount during the price negotiation, or even before talking about the flat price.

The minimum amount you may collect is $1 for option and $1 for exercise fee but this is seldom practiced.

This fee does depends on the market situation. Sometimes, buyers are reluctant to pay a high option fee ($1,000), especially if the purchase price of your flat is slightly above the market price as there is a risk the valuation maybe lower than the purchase price, and they couldn't afford to proceed with the purchase. As such, they may request that the option fee is between $200-$500.

You as the seller, should make it easier for the buyer to buy your flat especially if the buyer is using a loan from the HDB. As such, if you lower the cash outlay from the beginning, you are making your flat more attractive to many potential buyers.

However, if the buyer is using a bank loan, you may request that the total of both option fee and exercise fee is $5,000 …. with the option fee at maybe $500. And then you collect $4,500 as the exercise fee.

Now it's time for the paperwork. The prescribed OTP form shall be downloaded from the HDB InfoWeb (www.hdb.gov.sg)

A) You or the seller must fill in:

on Page 1 of the OTP:

    a. Option Date
    b. Flat Address
    c. Purchase Price (resale price of the flat)
    d. Option Fee (between $1 to $1,000)

e. Option Expiry Date (21 calendar days from the Option Date [including weekends and holidays]. e.g. if seller grants Option to you on 1 Aug, the Option will expire on 22 Aug at 4pm)

f. Names and NRIC numbers of all the sellers and buyers

OPTION TO PURCHASE

Option Date 1st August 2014

Flat address Blk 999, Pasir Ris Dr 14 #26-06 S(510999) *(Flat)*

1. Details

Purchase Price	$ 500,000 /—	("Purchase Price")
Option Fee (Up to a maximum of $1,000)	$ 500 /—	("Option Fee")
Option Expiry Date and Time (Date: State 21st calendar day starting after the Option Date)	On 22/08/14 (dd/mm/yy) at 4.00 p.m.	("Option Expiry")

		Name	NRIC Number
Seller	(1)	PAUL STANLEY	S1122334A
	(2)	GENE SIMMONS	S5566778B
	(3)		
	(4)		
Buyer	(1)	ACE FREHLEY	S0998877H
	(2)	PETER CRISS	S0665544J
	(3)		
	(4)		

B) the top half of page 8 of the OTP:

    a   Option Date

    b.   Flat Address

    c.   all sellers must sign on the OTP

    d.   a witness must sign on the OTP

(The witness can be the buyer's salesperson, or any person who is a Singapore citizen or Singapore Permanent Resident aged 21 years or above and not involved in the resale transaction)

Standard Contract for Resale of HDB Flat

Option Date : **1st August 2014**

Flat address : **Blk 999, Pasir Ris Dr 14 #26-06 S(510999)**

Signed by the Seller on the Option Date stated above.

Paul Stanley

Signed by Seller (1)

Gene Simmons

Signed by Seller (2)

Signed by Seller (3)

Signed by Seller (4)

Signature of Witness

Name: **Eddie Kramer**

NRIC: **S123456782**

*Our solicitors are

*Delete if not applicable.

ACCEPTANCE

This is the Acceptance referred to in Clause 8 of this Option.
We the Buyer accept the Seller's offer upon the terms set out in this Option.

Dated

Signed by Buyer (1)

Signed by Buyer (2)

Signed by Buyer (3)

Signed by Buyer (4)

Signature of Witness

Name:

NRIC :

Important Notice: Both buyers and sellers must declare the true resale price to HDB on the OTP. You cannot enter into any other agreements or arrangements that may cause the declared price to inflated or understated.

After both buyer and seller signed the OTP, the buyer will bring back the original copy. You can photocopy the OTP or you take a good picture of the OTP.

After that first meeting, the buyer will have to come back within 21 days to exercise the option and pay you the remaining agreed exercise fee.

Meanwhile, you can't sell your flat to any other buyers. At this stage, you should understand that you can't back out of this deal but the buyer can, but they will lose their option fee.

If the buyer is taking a loan and/or using his CPF to fund the flat, he will apply for a valuation report of the flat.

A valuer assigned by the HDB will call you for an appointment to come to your flat. It is your responsibility as the flat owner to allow the valuer to enter your flat for assessment, within 4 working days after the buyer submit the valuation request.

On the day of assessment, please let the valuer know the selling price of your flat.

If a buyer is buying your flat without taking any loan or a loan from the HDB, usually they will exercise to buy your flat within

14 days. Buyers are advised not to wait till the last hour to exercise the Option. You may also try to call the buyer or their agent on the estimated day they want to exercise the option.

If the buyer doesn't wants to buy your flat, they will let the Option expire, and you get to keep the option money.

You may then market the flat again to secure another buyer.

Note to BUYER:

You should use the Option period wisely and not rush into exercising the OTP. During this period, you must:

think and decide whether you really want to buy the flat.

if you are taking a bank loan, get a bank to issue you a Letter of Offer.

If the buyers decide to purchase the flat, they will exercise the option by doing these 3 things:-

1. sign the **Acceptance** portion in page 8 of the OTP.
2. deliver the signed OTP to you.
3. pay the option exercise fee.

Standard Contract for Resale of HDB Flat

Option Date : 1st August 2014
Flat address : Blk 999, Pasir Ris Dr 14 #26-06 S(510999)

Signed by the Seller on the Option Date stated above.

Paul Stanley

Signed by Seller (1)

Gene Simmons

Signed by Seller (2)

Signed by Seller (3)

Signed by Seller (4)

Signature of Witness

Name: Eddie Kramer
NRIC: S1234567 8 Z

Our solicitors are

Delete if not applicable.

ACCEPTANCE

This is the Acceptance referred to in Clause 6 of the Option.
We the Buyer accept the Seller's offer upon the terms set out in this Option.
Dated 22 August 2014

Signed by Buyer (1)

Peter Criss

Signed by Buyer (2)

Signed by Buyer (3)

Signed by Buyer (4)

Signature of Witness
Name: Bob Ezrin
NRIC: S98765432 A

Note : Please check with the buyers that they have <u>completed</u> the Buyers Resale Checklist. If they are taking a loan, the <u>date of issue</u> of the HDB HLE letter or the bank's Letter of Offer must be <u>before</u> the date of acceptance.

Once the buyer have exercised the OTP, both sellers and buyers have enter into a binding contract for the sale and purchase of the flat. Any party that backs out of this deal shall be liable for losses if the other party decides to claim compensation.

After the buyer exercised the option, you have to submit the sales to HDB and book for the 1st appointment. You have to do this within the time stipulated in the OTP.

Possible Scenarios

1. What happens when the valuation is below the purchase price? And the buyer couldn't afford to pay the cash over valuation.

You may proceed to find another buyer who is willing to pay your asking price. Or you could offer the current buyer to purchase your flat at the valuation price.

If both of you agrees to adjust the price, you will have to do on a new OTP. The buyer will also have to request for a new valuation. It means you will have to re-do the whole process again.

Do the buyers have to pay option fee again? YES. You and the buyers have to agree on the new option and exercise fee.

However, some sellers, out of goodwill, agrees to refund the 1st option fee and uses it for the 2nd option fee.

Note to buyers: If you decide not to buy after seller agrees to reduce his price but didn't want to refund the option fee, you will still have to pay an option fee at another different flat. You should take into consideration that you would have save a few thousand dollars when the seller reduces his selling price.

Buyer will have to pay for a new valuation report. Another valuer maybe assigned to assess the flat again.

At this stage, it is VERY IMPORTANT to let this valuer knows that this is the 2nd valuation. Let them know the previous selling price and the valuation then, and that this transaction was based on the previous valuation price.

2. What happens if the new valuation is below the selling price again?

In a rapidly declining market, this is possible. Then this becomes a "never ending" game. You decide if you want to repeat the above step again (reduce price, do a new contract and submit for valuation) but there is a risk the same thing will happen again.

Or you tell the buyer that you won't reduce the price anymore. Let the buyer decides if he's willing to pay Cash over Valuation.

Case Study:

A buyer bought a flat at $415K. The valuation comes out at $410K. Buyer doesn't want to pay Cash Over Valuation. So seller agree to reduce price and re-do everything. The 2nd valuation turns out to be $8K lower than the reduced selling price. This time, the seller doesn't wants to reduce his selling price, and the buyer can't wait any longer to buy a flat, so buyer exercised the option.

The buyer paid $8K cash over valuation instead of $5K only if they were to proceed with the 1st valuation.

CHAPTER 12

1ˢᵗ Appointment Date

Both of you should also agree on the 1ˢᵗ appointment date. When the buyer comes to exercise, both of you should come to an agreement on the 1ˢᵗ appointment date. If there is no prior agreement to delay the 1ˢᵗ appointment during the early stages of negotiation, the 1ˢᵗ appointment should be on the earliest possible date. You can check on the availability on the dates and time slots here:-

http://services2.hdb.gov.sg/webapp/BB24APPT1/WelcomeDate.jsp?date=201408

HDB 1ˢᵗ appointment time is usually in the morning from 8.45 am onwards.

Submission

Now it's the time to submit your resale purchase agreement to
HDB. Both buyers and sellers, at this point, should already agree
on when to submit the resale application to HDB. Both have to
submit within the time frame both of you have agreed. It is quite
common to agree on 30 days.

12. Application for HDB's approval

The Seller and Buyer will within ___30___ calendar days after the date of exercise of this Option, jointly apply to the HDB for its approval for the sale and purchase of the Flat.

13. Completion Date

Unless extended by the HDB, the Completion Date will be within 8 weeks after the date of the HDB's first appointment with the Seller and Buyer for the sale and purchase of the Flat.

14. Seller's obligations

14.1 The Seller must, within 7 working days after the request of the HDB or the Buyer's solicitor —

    (a) produce such documents;

    (b) sign such documents;

    (c) make such declarations; or

    (d) provide such information,

to the HDB or the Buyer's solicitor, as may be required to obtain the HDB's approval for the sale of the Flat.

14.2 The Seller must allow the HDB, or any of its authorised officers, to enter the Flat at any time in the day to check for unauthorised works or for such other purposes as may be required by the HDB.

14.3 The Seller must carry out such acts and sign such documents as the HDB or the Buyer's solicitor may direct to discharge any existing mortgage, charge, third party caveat or other encumbrance with respect to the Flat on or before completion.

14.4 The Seller must at his own cost before the Completion Date —

    (a) take down and remove all fixtures, fittings, structures or works done within the Flat not approved by the HDB;

    (b) repair and make good any resulting defects in the Flat; and

    (c) remove and dispose of all resulting surplus or waste materials from the Flat.

14.5 The Seller agrees to take such steps as the Buyer may reasonably request to help the Buyer obtain the HDB's approval for the purchase of the Flat.

14.6 If the sale proceeds are insufficient to —

    (a) refund any CPF moneys used by the Seller for the Flat together with accrued interest;

    (b) discharge in full any mortgage loan granted to the Seller by the HDB; or

    (c) repay any moneys owing by the Seller to the HDB,

the Seller must make such payments to the HDB, if the HDB so requires.

15. Buyer's obligations

15.1 The Buyer must, within 7 working days after the request of the HDB or the Seller's solicitor —

    (a) produce such documents;

    (b) sign such documents;

    (c) make such declarations; or

    (d) provide such information,

to the HDB or the Seller's solicitor, as may be required to obtain the HDB's approval for the purchase of the Flat.

Buyers and sellers will have to submit their portion of the application separately. Anyone can submit first. Their salesperson can submit on their behalf.

This is the link.:-

http://services2.hdb.gov.sg/webapp/BB31ERESALE3/BB31SMain

Once the first party has submitted his portion, the second party will have to do so within 7 days. Otherwise, it will lapse and you have to re-start the process.

The second party will be able to book the First Appointment (with the first party's consent) for the transaction.

Once the submission is successful, HDB will then assess the buyers' and sellers' eligibility to buy/sell the flat. HDB will send you a letter but if you didn't receive any, both buyers and sellers will be able to check on the status of their resale application via their MyHDBPage. Sometimes but seldom, HDB officers may call to seek clarifications.

If you need to change the First Appointment date, it can be done via MyHDBPage. Buyers and sellers can change the

First Appointment date only after they have received the First Appointment letter from HDB. If you need to change the 1st appointment date, please discuss and agree with the other party. Please take note that this is discouraged because if you change the appointment date, it does affects the timeline of the other party.

Flat Inspection by HDB

Before the 1st appointment, your flat will have to be inspected by your HDB Branch Office technical officers.

The seller will be informed of the inspection date in the 1st Appointment letter. The purpose of the inspection by the Branch is to check for unauthorised renovation works in the resale flat which may damage the HDB property and affect the structural stability of the flats/building.

If there is any unauthorised renovation works, it is your responsibility to rectify it.

1st appointment date

On the day of appointment, please turn up at the stipulated time at the HDB Hub. It is a good practise to be there at least 30 mins before your scheduled time.

You should also contact the buyer's party the night before and sent them a gentle reminder by SMS about the 1ˢᵗ appointment.

Documents seller needs to bring for the First Appointment:-

1. Original along with 1 photocopy of Identity Card(s) of seller(s)
2. Duplicate Lease, if it has been issued
3. Power of Attorney, if applicable

Please take note that you need to pay a conveyancing fee of $100-$400 to HDB after the 1st appointment.

The HDB will also explain to you the things you have to do before the completion date, which I will list later.

Both buyers and sellers can agree on the completion date here. It is scheduled about <u>six to eight</u> weeks from the date of the first appointment.

Note: If the buyer is taking a bank loan, the buyer should check with their conveyancing lawyers if they (the lawyers) are able to complete in 6 weeks……. should both buyers and sellers agree to complete in 6 weeks.

Result of your Resale Transaction

Within 2 weeks from the date of the first appointment, you will receive the approval letter from HDB.

You may also check the status of your resale application at My HDBPage.

<u>What You as the Seller Should Do Before the Completion Appointment</u>

1. Rectify any unauthorised renovation work carried out in the flat and inform the HDB Branch to confirm the rectification, if applicable
2. Terminate the GIRO account immediately for all payments pertaining to your flat
3. Clear all the outstanding payments if any as advised by the HDB resale officer:

Settle service and conservancy charges up to the day of resale completion

Pay the property tax up to the end of the year

What You Should Do Nearer to the Completion Appointment

1. Vacate the resale flat before the Date of Completion so that buyers can take possession of the resale flat after the Completion Appointment

2. Invite the buyers to inspect the resale flat

If sellers require a longer time to vacate the flat, they should discuss with the buyers and inform HDB resale officers to schedule the completion appointment at a later date.

Please note that if you have agreed to a particular completion date, and then re scheduled to a later date that will cause inconvenience to the buyer, you are <u>liable for compensation</u> for losses suffered by the buyer because of your decision to delay the completion.

Completion Appointment (Second Appointment)

The Completion Appointment is for the HDB to witness:-

1. The signing of the transfer document by the seller of the resale flat
2. The signing of the mortgage document/agreement by the buyer (if buyer is taking an HDB loan)

3. The handing over of the keys from you to the buyer (or to the buyer's lawyer if the buyer took a bank loan and engaged the bank's lawyer to act for the purchase) after:

4. to produce the official receipts to prove that you have paid the service and conservancy charges and property tax up to date

After the signing of the transfer documents, the flat is legally under the buyers names and thus buyers will be held responsible for any and all matters related to the flat.

<u>Sellers' Sales Proceeds (after the appointment)</u>

1. You will receive your cheque for the net sales proceeds, if any

2. HDB will arrange to refund the CPF monies to your CPF account. CPF refund will take place within 10 - 14 working days from the date of the completion appointment.

   Important Note: If you are buying another flat and would like the CPF to be refunded as soon as possible, please do inform your HDB resale officers as they may be able to assist with the request.

Other Possible Scenarios
Cancellation of resale application

The application will be cancelled if:

the resale is abortive for any reason whatsoever; or

the buyer and seller withdraw their application by giving notice in writing to the HDB; or

the buyer does not have sufficient CPF monies or cash to finance the purchase of the resale flat on the resale appointment date or fails to pay up the 10% of the purchase price in cash within 10 days from the resale appointment date and the balance at the date of completion; or

the information given in the Application Form by the seller/buyer is incorrect or the buyer/seller has suppressed any information required; or

the buyer/seller is ineligible to retain his application under the prevailing HDB's policies.

Note: If any buyers or sellers cancel the resale application, the other party that is inconvenienced should engage their own lawyers to claim for compensation. You have to engage your own private lawyers to do this even though the HDB may act for you as the conveyancing party.

Additional documents needed, if seller(s) is/are deceased

1. Death Certificate of Sellers and 3 photocopies
2. Grant of Letter of Administration/Probate, if applicable
3. Last Will of the deceased, if applicable
4. Order of Court to sanction the sale, if applicable

Additional documents needed if the sellers are divorced or separated

1. Deed of separation or Interim Judgment (previously known as Decree Nisi) and Certificate of Making Interim Judgment Final (previously known as Decree Nisi Absolute)
2. Order of Court, if any
3. any other documents of the divorce

Additional documents needed, for Singapore Permanent Resident households where seller(s) is/are bankrupt

1. Letter from the Official Assignee to consent to resale

Changes and New Rules
Temporary Extension of Stay

As from 22 July 2014, HDB have made it legal for sellers to stay in their flat temporarily after the completion. Previously after the sale/purchase of a resale flat is legally completed, the flat sellers are required to move out as the flat buyers become the new legal owners of the flat.

The move is part of HDB's regular review to respond to the needs of HDB resale flat sellers and buyers.

This move will facilitate sellers who are transiting to their next homes, including those who may need more time for renovation or those awaiting funds from the sale of their current flats.

Sellers will be able to negotiate with their buyers for a temporary extension of stay in their HDB flats, by up to 3 (three) months.

1. The temporary extension of stay is subject to the agreement of the flat buyers. As such, this is a REQUEST and not a RIGHT.
2. Sellers should take into consideration the selling price when you make such a request.

3. Buyers can deny the sellers the request for the extension of stay. However, if the extension of stay is important to the seller, seller may refuse to sell his flat to you.

4. Both buyers and sellers must negotiate on the terms of the extension of stay during the negotiating of the selling price. This terms should include the length of the stay and monetary compensation (if any).

5. Sellers must have committed to buy a completed housing unit (HDB flat or private residential property) in Singapore at the time of the resale application, i.e. they must have exercised an Option To Purchase or signed a Sale and Purchase Agreement.

6. The request for this Temporary Extension is to be submitted to HDB at the time of the resale application. An administrative fee of $20 (inclusive of GST) is payable by the flat buyers during the resale first appointment.

7. BUYERS should take note the start point for the computation of MOP will be set back by the period of the Temporary Extension of Stay. In addition, as legal owners of the flat, flat buyers must pay the Monthly Housing Loan Instalments and the Service & Conservancy Charges (without rebates) during the period of extension.

8. Both parties are encouraged to have a written agreement, signed by both the buyers and sellers, instead of just having a verbal agreement, to avoid future possible dispute. This

will be a private arrangement and they do not have to show their agreement to the HDB.

9. The extension of stay will automatically be terminated at the end of three months. Flat buyers must inform HDB via My HDBPage or contact our HDB Branch if they terminate the extension earlier. The computation of the MOP for the new owners will commence after the extension of stay is terminated.

In the event of any dispute, both parties should settle this amicably and not approach the HDB. If they can't settle on their own, they should approach their own lawyers.

For more comprehensive details, pls refer to the HDB InfoWeb or you could click this link:-

http://www.hdb.gov.sg/fi10/fi10321p.nsf/w/BuyResaleFlatTemporaryExtensionofStay?OpenDocument.

Acknowledgements

I hope you find the book an easy read but packed with information very useful to you. If you have successfully sold your flat by using the information here, I would like to congratulate you for closing a deal which saves you a couple of thousand dollars.

I would like to take this opportunity to thank the following people who have made the writing of this book possible:-

Allah, for blessing me with wisdom, strength and perseverance. Whenever I feel down in my business ventures, He is always there to encourage me whenever I turn to Him for guidance.

My parents, for imparting good values and for bringing me and my siblings up well.

My wife, Norra, for all the moral support that she has given me and for being there for me whenever I need her.

My previous and current managers/ mentors in the real estate industry: William Wong from RealStar Premier, Edward Yeo from ERA Property Navigators, Jasmi Talib from Global Millenium Holdings, Ayu Yanti from ERA Powerhouse Division and Adi Mesti Jadi from ERA Synergy Division.

Thanks to the many friends, family members, relatives, teammates, co-broke agents, mortgage brokers, conveyancing lawyers, present and past secretaries/personal assistants and most importantly, the CLIENTS who have given me their invaluable trust and support in me since 1996. I know I can count on them for many more good years.

Disclaimer

Those who wish to sell an HDB flat in the open resale market are free to decide whether they want to handle the sale on their own or to engage a salesperson to do it for them.

If you intend to do the sale of your flat on your own, you should be conversant with the property transaction process as you will not have the benefit and experience of a real estate consultant. You should read up all the information on HDB resale policies and procedures applicable to you.

Although the author and publisher have made every effort to ensure that the information in this book was correct at press time, the author and publisher do not assume and hereby disclaim any liability to any party for any loss, damage, or disruption caused by errors or omissions, whether such errors or omissions result from negligence, accident, or any other cause.

The information in this book is meant to supplement, not replace, any proper real estate training.

If you have successfully sold your flat on your own, you cannot act as a real estate agent for another person's flat. This is a serious offence in Singapore as all real estate agent have to be licenced and registered.

LICENSING OF ESTATE AGENTS AND REGISTRATION OF SALESPERSONS

Estate agents to be licensed

28.—(1) Subject to this Act, no person shall —

(a) exercise or carry on or advertise, notify or state that he exercises or carries on, or is willing to exercise or carry on, the business of doing estate agency work as an estate agent;

(b) act as an estate agent; or

(c) in any way hold himself out to the public as being ready to undertake, whether or not for payment or other remuneration (whether monetary or otherwise), estate agency work as an estate agent, unless he is a licensed estate agent.

(2) Any person who contravenes subsection (1) shall be guilty of an offence and shall be liable on conviction to a fine not exceeding $75,000, or to imprisonment for a term not exceeding 3 years or to both, and in the case of a continuing offence, to a further fine not exceeding $7,500 for every day or part thereof during which the offence continues after conviction.

(3) No fee, commission or reward in relation to anything done by a person in respect of an offence under this section shall be recoverable in any action, suit or matter by any person whomsoever.